Instant Nancy Web Development

Leverage the powerful and lightweight .NET-based Nancy Web Framework.

Christian Horsdal

BIRMINGHAM - MUMBAI

Instant Nancy Web Development

First published: September 2013

Production Reference: 1230913

Published by Packt Publishing Ltd.
Livery Place
35 Livery Street
Birmingham B3 2PB, UK.

ISBN 978-1-78328-391-0

www.packtpub.com

Credits

Author
Christian Horsdal

Reviewer
Michele Capra

Acquisition Editor
Antony Lowe

Commissioning Editor
Nikhil Chinnari

Technical Editor
Chandni Maishery

Copy Editors
Mradula Hegde
Alfida Paiva

Project Coordinator
Esha Thakker

Proofreader
Karen Estrada

Production Coordinator
Conidon Miranda

Cover Work
Conidon Miranda

Cover Image
Sheetal Aute

About the Author

Christian Horsdal is an independent consultant working with clients as an architect, consultant, and developer. He works with clients of all types, from small start-ups to large global companies.

Christian is an expert .NET architect and developer who mixes and matches commercial, open source, and tailor-made components in a quest to create simple and lean solutions that allow for quick and agile development.

Christian can be found online through his website `http://www.horsdal-consult.dk/`.

About the Reviewer

Michele Capra is an Italian software consultant, international speaker, and trainer on software development with Microsoft Technologies. He got his master's degree in Software Engineering in 2009 after working as a visiting researcher at Trinity College of Dublin. In the same year, he started working in the software industry and took part in a wide variety of software projects. He has been working for several financial institutions such as banks and funds, as well as start-ups. In these projects, he had the opportunity to learn and practice agile methodologies, for example, Test Driven Development, as well as to study Microsoft Technologies such as WPF, ASP.NET MVC, Windows Phone, and WinRT.

During his career, he has been speaking at several local .NET user-group events (such as WebAPI CodeCage, Windows Phone Refresh, C# Unleashed) as well as national (for example, WhyMCA) and international conferences (for example, Codemotion Berlin).

www.PacktPub.com

Support files, eBooks, discount offers and more

You might want to visit www.PacktPub.com for support files and downloads related to your book.

Did you know that Packt offers eBook versions of every book published, with PDF and ePub files available? You can upgrade to the eBook version at www.PacktPub.com and as a print book customer, you are entitled to a discount on the eBook copy. Get in touch with us at service@packtpub.com for more details.

At www.PacktPub.com, you can also read a collection of free technical articles, sign up for a range of free newsletters and receive exclusive discounts and offers on Packt books and eBooks.

http://PacktLib.PacktPub.com

Do you need instant solutions to your IT questions? PacktLib is Packt's online digital book library. Here, you can access, read and search across Packt's entire library of books.

Why Subscribe?

- Fully searchable across every book published by Packt
- Copy and paste, print and bookmark content
- On demand and accessible via web browser

Free Access for Packt account holders

If you have an account with Packt at www.PacktPub.com, you can use this to access PacktLib today and view nine entirely free books. Simply use your login credentials for immediate access.

Table of Contents

Preface

Welcome to *Instant Nancy Web Development*. I would like to start off by giving you a few motivations for using Nancy and touch upon the types of applications where I think Nancy really shines. These are personal opinions and others may not agree to it. That's OK. The point is, knowing that these are the motivations I have for using Nancy and that these are the situations where I'd use it, give you better context for reading this book.

The Nancy web framework (`http://nancyfx.org/`) was founded by Andreas Håkansson, who, along with Steven Robbins, maintains the project. Nancy was originally inspired by the Sinatra Ruby web frameworks, but is by no means a port.

Style matters

Before I get to the motivations for using Nancy, I want to digress for a bit. In this seemingly (or wannabe) rational realm of technology, we tend to focus a lot on the concrete and measurable things when we choose between one technology and the other, such as how do the features lists compare, how well does each cope with high volumes of load, and what is the total cost of ownership for each. We may end up with a chart or spreadsheet scoring each technology on multiple axis and calculating a final aggregate score which the answer to the choice. I think we too often miss an important component in these decisions, namely the style Why? Because style, in my experience, has a tremendous effect on the happiness of the developers working with the technology. Why does that matter? Well, apart from the basic good of people being happy, they are also more productive and more creative when they are happy. This is not too far from saying that a happier developer can save the development time and/or lead to a better product. That is quite tangible, and I argue that it has the potential benefit of choosing the more stylish or more aesthetically pleasing technology.

What is style then? It's a lot of small things, such as how the code looks line by line, how the framework makes you structure the code, and how terse versus explicit the code is.

As it turns out, Nancy's style really clicks for me. I find it fun and refreshing to work with. I hope the recipes in this book will make you feel the same way.

The super duper happy path

Nancy's declared ethos is to provide the super duper happy path; that is, it is a goal for Nancy to make anything you would want to do in a web application easy. To do this, Nancy employs a range of techniques and principles, such as:

  ▶ Small embedded **Domain Specific Language** (**DSL**) that makes your application code very short and very explicit at the same time.

  ▶ The other principle is **convention over configuration**. There are lots of things in Nancy applications that we don't need to be explicit about, because Nancy, out of the box, has sensible defaults. For instance, you don't have to configure all your Nancy modules (introduced in the recipes *Building and running your first Nancy application (Simple), Nancy testing – your first Nancy tests (Intermediate)*, and *Routes and model binding (Intermediate)*); instead, by convention, any Nancy module in your application code is automatically picked up by the framework.

  ▶ Everything, including the core pieces of the framework, can be extended with your custom extension or even swapped out completely, if needed. We will see examples of this in the recipes *Routes and model binding (Intermediate)* and *Content negotiation and more model binding (Advanced)*.

  ▶ Everything is highly testable. This is not a **Test Driven Development** (**TDD**) book, but I will say that I very much prefer to use TDD for the vast majority of my code, which means that for me, testability is a huge deal. Nancy allows a very nice TDD flow.

  ▶ Nancy is not tied to any particular platform beyond the client profile, **Base Class Library** (**BCL**). This means that Nancy runs on IIS, in a command-line application, in a WPF application, on Azure, and on Mono, just to name a few.

The result of the super duper happy path is that Nancy, for the most part, does exactly what I expected and wanted without much code. This gives Nancy applications a nice, lightweight feeling.

Sweet spot

The question remains, when to use Nancy? The short answer is that Nancy is suitable for all the .NET based web development. A slightly longer answer is that I find Nancy making the most sense for web applications with multiple clients. An example of this is a web application, where the main desktop UI is a single page JavaScript application (SPA), and which also has native apps for iOS, Android, and Windows Phone, a mobile version of the SPA, and may be, even a simple HTML UI for people who turn off JavaScript in their browsers. Such an application calls for an architecture where the backend exposes a common API over HTTP that all the clients use. The nice embedded HTTP DSL and the content negotiation features make Nancy a perfect fit for building an HTTP based API.

The running example used in the book is a simple to-do application with two clients, an SPA and a very simple server-side generated HTML UI. The Nancy to-do application will be ready to support other clients, for example, mobiles. The focus, though, will be on building the backend part with Nancy, using TDD. The client-side pieces of software are mainly out of scope of this book. Therefore the SPA client, we will use, is the well-known Backbone TodoMVC application (`http://todomvc.com/architecture-examples/backbone/`). The details of the code of the Backbone TodoMVC application and of any mobile clients are out of scope.

What this book covers

Building and running your first Nancy application (Simple) shows you how to get from zero to hello world with Nancy in no time. At the same time, you will see an example of the part of Nancy you will probably be using the most in real applications.

Nancy testing – your first Nancy tests (Intermediate) gets you started down the path of sound-test-driven development with Nancy. The emphasis is not on TDD, but on Nancy, and along the way, you will see how Nancy treats tests as first-class citizens.

Routes and model binding (Intermediate) walks you through how to easily receive data from client side code in your routes. You will also dig a level deeper into how to set up the routes with Nancy.

Taking a dependency – introducing the bootstrapper (Intermediate) shows you how Nancy lets you handle configuration in code with the bootstrapper. This recipe will also show you just how easy Nancy makes it to inject the dependencies into your application code without giving up any control or any testability.

Content negotiation and more model binding (Advanced) takes you a level deeper into model binding, and furthermore, delves into the concept of content negotiation. You will see how you give client-side code a great amount of flexibility while maintaining a nice separation of concerns on the server side.

Adding views (Intermediate) shows you how to add server-side-rendered Razor views to your Nancy application, and how to configure Nancy to use a variety of other view engines.

Adding static content (Intermediate) shows you how to serve static content easily, following Nancy's default conventions, and how to augment those conventions to suit your own needs.

Hosting Nancy on the Cloud (Intermediate) shows you how to deploy your Nancy application to the AppHarbor PaaS cloud service, and discusses how to deploy Windows Azure. In both the cases, very little work needs to be done.

Handling cross-cutting concerns – Before, After, and Error hooks (Intermediate) shows you how to easily hook into Nancy's request and error handling pipelines in order to add your own custom steps.

Authenticating users (Intermediate) shows how to add Twitter and other third-party authentication to your Nancy application with only a little bit of work. Furthermore, you will be introduced to how Nancy helps you do authorization on a module or route basis.

Separating applications and hosting (Advanced) explains the notion of hosting in a Nancy application and shows you how to easily set up your application such that it can be run under several different types of hosting.

Using async handlers (Advanced) shows you how to turn existing synchronous request handlers into async request handlers. Doing this involves just a few easy steps and can potentially improve your application's scalabilty.

What you need for this book

All you will need to code along with the recipes is a Windows box with Visual Studio 2012 Express for Web (or a "bigger") edition, a working knowledge of C#, and of the Web.

Who this book is for

The book is for any curious .NET developer who is keen to find out what all the fuss concerning Nancy, Sinatra, and other lightweight web frameworks is about.

Conventions

In this book, you will find a number of styles of text that distinguish between different kinds of information. Here are some examples of these styles, and an explanation of their meaning.

Code words in text are shown as follows: "We can set up a route by use of the Get property."

A block of code is set as follows:

```
public class Hello : NancyModule
{
  public Hello()
  {
    Get["/"] = _ => "Hello!";
  }
}
```

When we wish to draw your attention to a particular part of a code block, the relevant lines or items are set in bold:

```
Get["/"] = _ =>
  Negotiate
  .WithModel(todoStore.GetAll().Where(todo =>
    todo.userName == Context.CurrentUser.UserName)
    .ToArray())
  .WithView("Todos");
```

Any command-line input or output is written as follows:

```
PS > Install-Package Nancy
```

New terms and **important words** are shown in bold. Words that you see on the screen, in menus or dialog boxes for example, appear in the text like this: "click on **add** you get an Internal Server Error ".

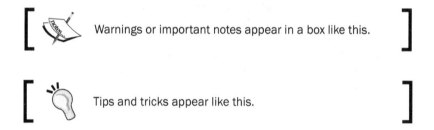

Warnings or important notes appear in a box like this.

Tips and tricks appear like this.

Reader feedback

Feedback from our readers is always welcome. Let us know what you think about this book—what you liked or may have disliked. Reader feedback is important for us to develop titles that you really get the most out of.

To send us general feedback, simply send an e-mail to feedback@packtpub.com, and mention the book title via the subject of your message.

If there is a book that you need and would like to see us publish, please send us a note in the **SUGGEST A TITLE** form on www.packtpub.com or e-mail suggest@packtpub.com.

If there is a topic that you have expertise in and you are interested in either writing or contributing to a book, see our author guide on www.packtpub.com/authors.

Customer support

Now that you are the proud owner of a Packt book, we have a number of things to help you to get the most from your purchase.

Downloading the example code

You can download the example code files for all Packt books you have purchased from your account at `http://www.PacktPub.com`. If you purchased this book elsewhere, you can visit `http://www.PacktPub.com/support` and register to have the files e-mailed directly to you.

Errata

Although we have taken every care to ensure the accuracy of our content, mistakes do happen. If you find a mistake in one of our books—maybe a mistake in the text or the code—we would be grateful if you would report this to us. By doing so, you can save other readers from frustration and help us improve subsequent versions of this book. If you find any errata, please report them by visiting `http://www.packtpub.com/support`, selecting your book, clicking on the **errata submission form** link, and entering the details of your errata. Once your errata are verified, your submission will be accepted and the errata will be uploaded on our website, or added to any list of existing errata, under the Errata section of that title. Any existing errata can be viewed by selecting your title from `http://www.packtpub.com/support`.

Piracy

Piracy of copyright material on the Internet is an ongoing problem across all media. At Packt, we take the protection of our copyright and licenses very seriously. If you come across any illegal copies of our works, in any form, on the Internet, please provide us with the location address or website name immediately so that we can pursue a remedy.

Please contact us at `copyright@packtpub.com` with a link to the suspected pirated material.

We appreciate your help in protecting our authors, and our ability to bring you valuable content.

Questions

You can contact us at `questions@packtpub.com` if you are having a problem with any aspect of the book, and we will do our best to address it.

Instant Nancy Web Development

Welcome to *Instant Nancy Web Development*! Nancy is a lightweight and fun-to-work-with web framework. At the same time, it is a fully featured web framework that lets you write the most modern day web applications and web APIs. Nancy is written in and for C# and runs on .NET as well as Mono.

Building and running your first Nancy application (Simple)

In this recipe, you will write your very first Nancy application. It will not do much, but you will see just how easy it is to get started with Nancy.

Getting ready

Before diving in and building your first Nancy application, there are a couple of things you will need. First and foremost, I'll assume that for this recipe and the rest of the book, you have Visual Studio 2012 Express for Web or a higher version installed, and you have the NuGet Package Manager extension installed and up-to-date. If not, go to `http://www.microsoft.com/visualstudio/eng/products/visual-studio-express-for-web#product-express-web`, download and install Visual Studio, and then go to **Tools | Extension and Updates...** dialog and make sure **NuGet Package Manager** is up-to-date.

How to do it...

Going from zero to hello world with Nancy is as simple as following these steps:

1. Open Visual Studio.

2. Create a new empty ASP.NET project by navigating to **File | New Project...** and selecting the **ASP.NET Empty Web Application** template under **Visual C# | Web**. Let's call the project `HelloNancy`.

3. Open **Package Manager Console**. At the prompt, type the following line of code:

   ```
   PM> Install-Package Nancy.Hosting.Aspnet
   ```

   The previous line of code will produce an output similar to this:

   ```
   Attempting to resolve dependency 'Nancy (≥ 0.17.1)'.
   Installing 'Nancy 0.17.1'.
   Successfully installed 'Nancy 0.17.1'.
   Installing 'Nancy.Hosting.Aspnet 0.17.1'.
   Successfully installed 'Nancy.Hosting.Aspnet 0.17.1'.
   Adding 'Nancy 0.17.1' to HelloNancy.
   Successfully added 'Nancy 0.17.1' to HelloNancy.
   Adding 'Nancy.Hosting.Aspnet 0.17.1' to HelloNancy.
   Successfully added 'Nancy.Hosting.Aspnet 0.17.1' to
   HelloNancy.
   ```

4. Add a new C# file at the root of the project. Call it `HelloModule` and put the following code in it:

   ```
   namespace HelloNancy
   {
     using Nancy;

     public class HelloModule : NancyModule
     {
       public HelloModule()
       {
         Get ["/"] = _ => "Hello Nancy World";
       }
     }
   }
   ```

5. Press *F5* and marvel at the fact that you've just created your first Nancy application. When you run this application, you should see something rather close to this:

How it works...

Let's take a quick look at what happened in the previous section. The interesting parts are steps 3 and 4.

In step 3, you installed the `Nancy.Hosting.Aspnet` package and the Nancy `NuGet` packages into the newly created `HelloNancy` project. This will download the `Nancy` assembly and the `Nancy.Hosting.Aspnet` assembly from the NuGet gallery, and add references to both in the `HelloNancy` project. The Nancy assembly is the Nancy framework, and the `Nancy.Hosting.Aspnet` assembly is an adapter for running the Nancy application on top of ASP.NET. In Nancy terms, this is called hosting Nancy on ASP.NET. Hosting is the subject of the *Separating application and hosting (Advanced)* recipe.

In step 4, you created a `NancyModule` class. Nancy modules are at the heart of Nancy applications. They are used to define which routes the application accepts and how it handles each one. For instance, the `NancyModule` class in step 4 defines one route and a handler for that route. This is done in the following line:

```
Get["/"] = _ => "Hello Nancy World";
```

This tells Nancy that an HTTP GET request to the route `"/"` should be handled by the lambda expression on the right-hand side of the `=` sign. In other words, each time Nancy receives an HTTP GET `"/"`, it calls the following line of code:

```
_ => "Hello Nancy World";
```

In the previous line of code, the lambda expression takes one parameter called `_`. It doesn't use the parameter for anything but simply returns the `Hello Nancy World` string back to Nancy. Since nothing went wrong, Nancy will create an HTTP `200 OK` response with `Hello Nancy World` in the body and return it as the response to HTTP GET `"/"`.

On a side note, I like to adopt the convention that whenever a parameter in a lambda is not used in the body of the lambda, I call it `_`. I like this because visually it makes the parameter almost disappear, so I instantly know that it is not used. On the other hand, if it is used, I will always give it a name. I will be using `_` throughout this book for unused parameters.

On start-up, Nancy will find all Nancy modules in all loaded assemblies and instantiate each one. In the case of the module from step 4 in the previous section, the constructor containing the route definition discussed previously is run.

There's more...

This was just a very quick peek into how Nancy applications are written. Through the rest of the book, we will see many more features of Nancy, which will put you in a position to write real Nancy applications and not just `Hello World`.

Also, you should be aware of the Nancy documentation, which can be found at `https://github.com/NancyFx/Nancy/wiki/Documentation`, and the Nancy demos along with the Nancy source code at `https://github.com/NancyFx/Nancy/tree/master/src`.

Nancy testing – your first Nancy tests (Intermediate)

In this section, you will see how to start writing tests for your Nancy application. Throughout the book, I will write tests before implementation, following the red, green, refactor cycle of TDD. Consequently, you will see how to test many aspects of Nancy applications. This section just gets you started to using Nancy's testing features.

Getting ready

Before writing your first Nancy test, you'll need a unit testing framework and a test runner. I will be using xUnit.net (`http://xunit.codeplex.com/`), but you can use whichever .NET testing framework that suits you.

How to do it...

The following steps will help you write tests for your Nancy application:

1. Open Visual Studio.

2. Create a new empty C# ASP.NET project and call it `TodoNancy`.

3. Create a new C# Class Library project and call it `TodoNancyTests`.

4. Go to **Package Manager Console** and write the following line of code in it:

   ```
   PM> Install-Package Nancy.Testing TodoNancyTests
   ```

5. This pulls down the `Nancy.Testing NuGet` package and installs it into the `TodoNancyTests` project. This package contains Nancy's support for testing.

6. Go back to the **Package Manager Console** and write the following line of code to install the xUnit test framework:

   ```
   PM> Install-Package xunit TodoNancyTests
   ```

7. Add a project reference to the `TodoNancy` project in the `TodoNancyTests` project. This is done by right-clicking on **References** under the **TodoNancyTests** project, choosing **Add Reference...**, and in the dialog that opens, find the **TodoNancy** project under **Solution | Projects**. Your solution should now look like the following screenshot:

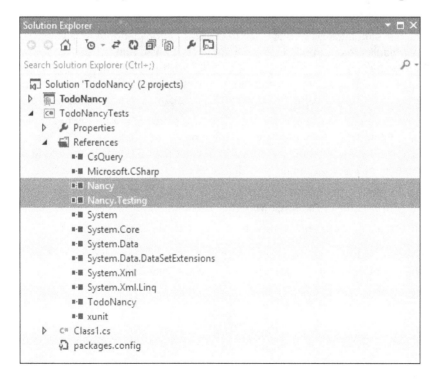

8. There is a file called **Class1.cs** in the **TodoNancyTests** project. Rename it to `HomeModuleTests` and put the following code in it:

```
namespace TodoNancyTests
{
  using Nancy;
  using Nancy.Testing;
  using Xunit;

  public class HomeModuleTests
  {
    [Fact]
    public void Should_answer_200_on_root_path()
    {
      var sut = new Browser(new
        DefaultNancyBootstrapper());

      var actual = sut.Get("/");

      Assert.Equal(HttpStatusCode.OK, actual.StatusCode);
    }
  }
}
```

9. This test simulates HTTP `GET` `"/"` to our Nancy application. We have not added any modules to our application, so it should not pass. Run the test and watch it fail. The test can be run using the xUnit.net test runner for Visual Studio (`http://visualstudiogallery.msdn.microsoft.com/463c5987-f82b-46c8-a97e-b1cde42b9099`) or using TestDriven.NET (`http://testdriven.net/`).

10. Note the variable naming in the test. They are a part of another set of conventions I like to follow. The `sut` variable is the thing being tested. It is short for system under test. The `actual` variable is the result of what the test does to the production code. Consequently, `actual` usually holds the value asserted at the end of the test.

11. Add the Nancy framework to the `TodoNancy` project, and enable running on top of ASP.NET by going to **Package Manager Console** and typing in this command:

```
PM> Install-Package Nancy.Hosting.Aspnet TodoNancy
```

12. To make the test pass, we need to add a new C# file to the root of the `TodoNancy` project. Let's call it `HelloModule` and add the following code to it:

```
namespace TodoNancy
{
  using Nancy;
```

```
public class HomeModule : NancyModule
{
  public HomeModule()
  {
    Get["/"] = _ => HttpStatusCode.OK;
  }
}
}
```

13. Your **Solution Explorer** should now look more or less as the following screenshot:

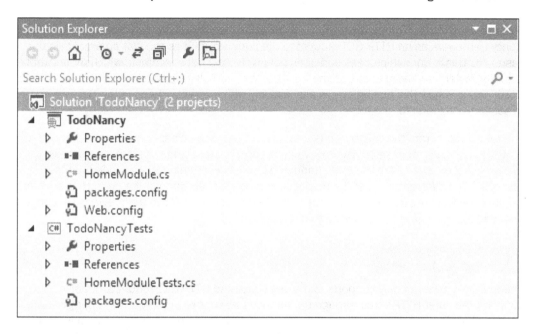

14. Re-run the test from beginning and watch it succeed.

How it works...

Congratulations! You just created your first piece of the Nancy application code in a test-first fashion.

Taking a closer look at the test code, the first thing to notice is the following line of code:

```
var sut = new Browser(new DefaultNancyBootstrapper());
```

This creates an instance of the `Browser` class from the `Nancy.Testing` namespace, which is an essential type of object while testing Nancy modules. The `Browser` type allows making calls that simulate real HTTP requests without neither the Nancy framework, nor your application code knowing the difference. Furthermore, these simulated requests are made without actually going through the network stack. This is important because it gives you the opportunity to write tests that are both fast and run against the API you expose to clients; for example, browsers.

The next thing to note is the following line of code:

```
var actual = sut.Get("/");
```

This line uses the `Get` method of the `Browser` object, which will create what appears to the Nancy framework as an HTTP GET request to the path provided as the first argument—in this case `"/"`. This is done in-process and does not involve the network stack, which means that it is a lot faster and easier to set up than tests that make full-fledged real HTTP requests. Also worth noting is how this testing syntax aligns nicely with the syntax used in the Nancy module to set up the handler for the route.

The return value from the call to `Get` is a `BrowserResponse` class—another class from the `Nancy.Testing` namespace. The `BrowserResponse` class gives the tests the access to everything returned from the route handler as well as everything Nancy added to that response. The different parts of the response can be reached through the properties such as `StatusCode`, `Headers`, `Cookies`, and `Body`. In the test we wrote in the previous section, we just read `StatusCode` and asserted that it was `200 OK`.

There's more...

The `Browser` type not only supports in making simulated HTTP `GET` requests but also supports the other HTTP verbs through the methods `Post`, `Delete`, `Put`, `Patch`, `Options`, and `Head`, it. Each of these methods is used in a similar fashion to `Get`. In later recipes, we will see how to specify the body of the simulated HTTP request; for example, a call to `Post`. We will also see how to set HTTP headers for calls made through the `Browser` objects.

Furthermore, if you want a test to make a sequence of calls to your API, you can do this by using the `Then` method on the `BrowserResponse` class. The `Then` method allows you to chain simulated HTTP requests one after the other in the following manner:

```
var actual = sut.Get("/").Then.Get("/foo");
```

Lastly, `Nancy.Testing` includes some convenient methods for asserting against the contents of the body of responses when the body is either JSON, XML, or HTML. We will see these features in the upcoming recipes as we will actually start returning something from our route handlers.

Routes and model binding (Intermediate)

Starting from this recipe, we will slightly speed things up by leaving out details of Visual Studio usage, and in some cases only code snippets will be shown instead of full classes. It should be clear from the concepts where the snippets fit, and they can be further investigated in the code downloads for individual recipes.

For the sake of brevity, I will also show several tests in just one step and also the necessary production code in one go. Though, I strongly recommend that you stick to good TDD practices, and add the tests one at a time and make each one pass before moving on to the next.

In this recipe, we take a look at how to handle the other HTTP verbs apart from GET and how to work with dynamic routes such as /custumer/42, where 42 is the customer ID. We will also look at how to work with JSON data and how to do model binding.

In this recipe, we will see the Todo application, which is the running example of the book, take shape. In fact at the end of this recipe, you will have a backend—if hooked up correctly—that works with the canonical JavaScript library todo samples. The downloadable code for this recipe is attached with the backbone.js todo sample.

Getting ready

This section builds on the previous section and assumes you have the TodoNancy and TodoNancyTests projects all set up.

How to do it...

The following steps will help you to handle the other HTTP verbs and work with dynamic routes:

1. Open the TodoNancy Visual Studio solution.
2. Add a new class to the NancyTodoTests project, call it TodosModulesTests, and fill this test code for a GET and a POST route into it:

```
public class TodosModuleTests
{
  private Browser sut;
  private Todo aTodo;
  private Todo anEditedTodo;

  public TodosModuleTests()
  {
    TodosModule.store.Clear();
    sut = new Browser(new DefaultNancyBootstrapper());
```

```
        aTodo = new Todo
        {
          title = "task 1", order = 0, completed = false
        };
        anEditedTodo = new Todo()
        {
          id = 42, title = "edited name", order = 0,
            completed = false
        };
    }

    [Fact]
    public void
      Should_return_empty_list_on_get_when_no_todos_
      have_been_posted()
    {
      var actual = sut.Get("/todos/");

      Assert.Equal(HttpStatusCode.OK, actual.StatusCode);
      Assert.Empty(actual.Body.DeserializeJson<Todo[]>());
    }

    [Fact]
    public void
      Should_return_201_create_when_a_todo_is_posted()
    {
      var actual = sut.Post("/todos/",  with =>
        with.JsonBody(aTodo));

      Assert.Equal(HttpStatusCode.Created,
        actual.StatusCode);
    }

    [Fact]
    public void
      Should_not_accept_posting_to_with_duplicate_id()
    {
      var actual = sut.Post("/todos/", with =>
        with.JsonBody(anEditedTodo))
        .Then
        .Post("/todos/", with =>
          with.JsonBody(anEditedTodo));

      Assert.Equal(HttpStatusCode.NotAcceptable,
        actual.StatusCode);
```

```
        }

        [Fact]
        public void Should_be_able_to_get_posted_todo()
        {
          var actual = sut.Post("/todos/", with =>
            with.JsonBody(aTodo) )
            .Then
            .Get("/todos/");

          var actualBody =
            actual.Body.DeserializeJson<Todo[]>();
          Assert.Equal(1, actualBody.Length);
          AssertAreSame(aTodo, actualBody[0]);
        }

        private void AssertAreSame(Todo expected, Todo actual)
        {
          Assert.Equal(expected.title, actual.title);
          Assert.Equal(expected.order, actual.order);
          Assert.Equal(expected.completed, actual.completed);
        }
      }
```

3. The main thing to notice new in these tests is the use of `actual.Body.DesrializeJson<Todo[]>()`, which takes the `Body` property of the `BrowserResponse` type, assumes it contains JSON formatted text, and then deserializes that string into an array of `Todo` objects.

4. At the moment, these tests will not compile. To fix this, add this `Todo` class to the `TodoNancy` project as follows:

```
public class Todo
{
  public long id { get; set; }
  public string title { get; set; }
  public int order { get; set; }
  public bool completed { get; set; }
}
```

5. Then, go to the `TodoNancy` project, and add a new C# file, call it `TodosModule`, and add the following code to body of the new class:

```
public static Dictionary<long, Todo> store = new
  Dictionary<long, Todo>();
```

6. Run the tests and watch them fail. Then add the following code to `TodosModule`:

```
public TodosModule() : base("todos")
{
  Get["/"] = _ => Response.AsJson(store.Values);

  Post["/"] = _ =>
  {
    var newTodo = this.Bind<Todo>();
    if (newTodo.id == 0)
      newTodo.id = store.Count + 1;

    if (store.ContainsKey(newTodo.id))
      return HttpStatusCode.NotAcceptable;

    store.Add(newTodo.id, newTodo);
    return Response.AsJson(newTodo)
                  .WithStatusCode(HttpStatusCode.Created);
  };
}
```

7. The previous code adds two new handlers to our application. One handler for the GET `"/todos/"` HTTP and the other handler for the POST `"/todos/"` HTTP. The GET handler returns a list of `todo` items as a JSON array. The POST handler allows for creating new `todos`. Re-run the tests and watch them succeed.

8. Now let's take a closer look at the code. Firstly, note how adding a handler for the POST HTTP is similar to adding handlers for the GET HTTP. This consistency extends to the other HTTP verbs too. Secondly, note that we pass the `"todos"` string to the `base` constructor. This tells Nancy that all routes in this module are related to `/todos`. Thirdly, notice the `this.Bind<Todo>()` call, which is Nancy's data binding in action; it deserializes the body of the POST HTTP into a `Todo` object.

9. Now go back to the `TodosModuleTests` class and add these tests for the PUT and DELETE HTTP as follows:

```
[Fact]
public void Should_be_able_to_edit_todo_with_put()
{
  var actual = sut.Post("/todos/", with => with.JsonBody(aTodo))
    .Then
    .Put("/todos/1", with => with.JsonBody(anEditedTodo))
    .Then
    .Get("/todos/");
```

```
      var actualBody = actual.Body.DeserializeJson<Todo[]>();
      Assert.Equal(1, actualBody.Length);
      AssertAreSame(anEditedTodo, actualBody[0]);
  }


  [Fact]
  public void Should_be_able_to_delete_todo_with_delete()
  {
      var actual = sut.Post("/todos/", with => with.Body(aTodo.
  ToJSON()))
          .Then
          .Delete("/todos/1")
          .Then
          .Get("/todos/");

      Assert.Equal(HttpStatusCode.OK, actual.StatusCode);
      Assert.Empty(actual.Body.DeserializeJson<Todo[]>());
  }
```

10. After watching these tests fail, make them pass by adding this code to the constructor of `TodosModule`:

```
      Put["/{id}"] = p =>
      {
        if (!store.ContainsKey(p.id))
          return HttpStatusCode.NotFound;

        var updatedTodo = this.Bind<Todo>();
        store[p.id] = updatedTodo;
        return Response.AsJson(updatedTodo);
      };

      Delete["/{id}"] = p =>
      {
        if (!store.ContainsKey(p.id))
          return HttpStatusCode.NotFound;

        store.Remove(p.id);
        return HttpStatusCode.OK;
      };
```

11. All tests should now pass.

12. Take a look at the routes to the new handlers for the `PUT` and `DELETE` HTTP. Both are defined as `"/{id}"`. This will match any route that starts with `/todos/` and then something more that appears after the trailing `/`, such as `/todos/42` and the `{id}` part of the route definition is `42`. Notice that both these new handlers use their `p` argument to get the ID from the route in the `p.id` expression. Nancy lets you define very flexible routes. You can use any regular expression to define a route. All named parts of such regular expressions are put into the argument for the handler. The type of this argument is `DynamicDictionary`, which is a special Nancy type that lets you look up parts via either `indexers` (for example, `p["id"]`) like a dictionary, or dot notation (for example, `p.id`) like other dynamic C# objects.

There's more...

In addition to the handlers for `GET`, `POST`, `PUT`, and `DELETE`, which we added in this recipe, we can go ahead and add handler for `PATCH` and `OPTIONS` by following the exact same pattern.

Out of the box, Nancy automatically supports `HEAD` and `OPTIONS` for you. To handle the `HEAD` HTTP request, Nancy will run the corresponding `GET` handler but only return the headers. To handle `OPTIONS`, Nancy will inspect which routes you have defined and respond accordingly.

Taking a dependency – introducing the bootstrapper (Intermediate)

In this recipe, we will start persisting the `Todo` objects added to `TodoNancy` through `POST` requests to a data store. We will also persist edits done through `PUT` requests and remove `Todos` from the data store, which are removed through `DELETE` requests. The implementation of the data store for the `Todo` objects is not very interesting. It can easily be done against any database and is left as an exercise for you. For inspiration, you can have a look at the code download for this recipe where the data store is implemented against MongoDB.

This recipe will show you how Nancy uses dependency injection to make taking dependencies in modules easy and how to use a Nancy `bootstrapper` to configure these dependencies if necessary.

Getting ready

This recipe builds on the previous recipe and assumes that you have the `TodoNancy` and `TodoNancyTests` projects all set up.

How to do it...

The following steps will show you how to manage the dependencies your modules may have:

1. First, we add a new file to the `NancyTodoTests` project, call it `DataStoreTests`, and add the tests below to it. These tests use the `FakeItEasy` mock library (`https://github.com/FakeItEasy/FakeItEasy`), which is a straightforward and flexible mocking framework, that I find complements the style of `Nancy.Testing` well.

```
public class DataStoreTests
{
  private readonly IDataStore fakeDataStore;
  private Browser sut;
  private readonly Todo aTodo;

  public DataStoreTests()
  {
    fakeDataStore = A.Fake<IDataStore>();
    sut = new Browser( with =>
    {
      with.Dependency(fakeDataStore);
      with.Module<TodosModule>();
    });

    aTodo = new Todo() {id = 5, title = "task 10", order
      = 100, completed = true };
  }

  [Fact]
  public void Should_store_posted_todos_in_datastore()
  {
    sut.Post("/todos/", with => with.JsonBody(aTodo));

    AssertCalledTryAddOnDataStoreWtih(aTodo);
  }

  private void AssertCalledTryAddOnDataStoreWtih(Todo
    expected)
  {
    A.CallTo(() =>
      fakeDataStore.TryAdd(A<Todo>
        .That.Matches(actual =>
          {
```

```
                    Assert.Equal(expected.title, actual.title);
                    Assert.Equal(expected.order, actual.order);
                    Assert.Equal(expected.completed,
                      actual.completed);
                     return true;
                   }
       )))
              .MustHaveHappened();
         }
```

2. This test uses a HTTP POST method to send a new `todo` object to our `TodoNancy` application and then asserts that a similar `Todo` object was added to the fake data store created in the constructor. The way the `Browser` object is created in the constructor is of special interest. Until now, we have created `Browser` objects based on `DefaultNancyBootstrapper`. From now on, we will need to take a bit more control over how the `Browser` object is set up. In particular, we will set up the fake data store object, `fakeDataStore`, as a dependency and we tell Nancy to only look for one module, namely `TodosModule`.

3. To satisfy this test, we will first add an `IDataStore` interface to the `TodoNancy` project as shown here:

```
public interface IDataStore
{
   IEnumerable<Todo> GetAll();
   long Count { get; }
   bool TryAdd(Todo todo);
   bool TryRmove(int id);
   bool TryUpdate(Todo todo);
}
```

4. Then, we need to change the `TodosModule` class so that it takes a dependency on `IDataStore`:

```
public TodosModule(IDataStore todoStore) :
   base("todos")
```

5. And lastly, we need to change the handler for POST in `TodosModule` to use `todoStores` as follows:

```
Post["/"] = _ =>
{
   var newTodo = this.Bind<Todo>();
   if (newTodo.id == 0)
      newTodo.id = todoStore.Count + 1;

   if (!todoStore.TryAdd(newTodo))
```

```
        return HttpStatusCode.NotAcceptable;

    return Response.AsJson(newTodo)
        .WithStatusCode(HttpStatusCode.Created);
};
```

6. We then move on to test the use of IDataStore by the other handlers. The implementation details of these are left to you, the reader, or can be found in code download for this recipe. Such a test will drive changes to the TodosModule class so that it becomes as follows:

```
public class TodosModule : NancyModule
{
    public static Dictionary<long, Todo> store = new
        Dictionary<long, Todo>();

    public TodosModule(IDataStore todoStore) :
        base("todos")
    {
        Get["/"] = _ => Response.AsJson(todoStore.GetAll());

        Post["/"] = _ =>
        {
            var newTodo = this.Bind<Todo>();
            if (newTodo.id == 0)
                newTodo.id = todoStore.Count + 1;

            if (!todoStore.TryAdd(newTodo))
                return HttpStatusCode.NotAcceptable;

            return Response.AsJson(newTodo)
                .WithStatusCode(HttpStatusCode.Created);
        };

        Put["/{id}"] = p =>
        {
            var updatedTodo = this.Bind<Todo>();
            if (!todoStore.TryUpdate(updatedTodo))
                return HttpStatusCode.NotFound;

            return Response.AsJson(updatedTodo);
        };

        Delete["/{id}"] = p =>
        {
```

```
      if (!todoStore.TryRmove(p.id))
        return HttpStatusCode.NotFound;

      return HttpStatusCode.OK;
    };
  }
}
```

7. At this point, our `NancyTodos` application is ported over to use the `IDataStore` interface to store the `todo` object, but there is still no implementation of the `IDataStore` interface; so, if you try to run the application or any of the other tests, you get a very long exception message at the bottom of which you find this:

```
Nancy.TinyIoc.TinyIoCResolutionException
Unable to resolve type: TodoNancy.IDataStore    at Nancy.TinyIoc.
TinyIoCContainer.ResolveInternal(TypeRegistra
tion registration, NamedParameterOverloads parameters,
ResolveOptions options)    at
Nancy.TinyIoc.TinyIoCContainer.ConstructType(Type
requestedType, Type implementationType, ConstructorInfo
constructor, NamedParameterOverloads parameters,
ResolveOptions options)
```

8. This tells us that Nancy is—naturally—not able to find an implementation of `IDataStore`. This in turn means Nancy will not start up the application because it needs an `IDataStore` implementation for the `TodosModule` class.

9. Any implementation of `IDataStore` will do and I will leave this to you. In the code for download, you can find an implementation that works against the MongoDB (`http://www.mongodb.org/`) document database. There is a problem though. The `IDataStore` MongoDB implementation needs a connection string in order to connect to a MongoDB server. Nancy cannot know this connection string, so our application code needs to provide the connection string to the MongoDB data store. This kind of setup in Nancy applications belongs in a bootstrapper. In our case, we extend the default Nancy bootstrapper in order to preserve most of the defaults and just a little bit extra as follows:

```
public class Bootstrapper : DefaultNancyBootstrapper
{
  protected override void
    ConfigureApplicationContainer(TinyIoCContainer
    container)    {
      base.ConfigureApplicationContainer(container);

      var mongoDataStore = new
      MongoDataStore("mongodb://localhost:27010/todos");
      container.Register<IDataStore>(mongoDataStore);
  }
```

10. The `TodosModuleTests` function needs its setup code tweaked a little bit to become as follows:

```
public TodosModuleTests()
{
  var database =
  MongoDatabase.Create("mongodb://localhost:27017
    /todos");
  database.Drop();

  sut = new Browser(new Bootstrapper());
  aTodo = new Todo
  {
    title = "task 1", order = 0, completed = false
  };
  anEditedTodo = new Todo()
  {
    id = 42, title = "edited name", order = 0,
      completed = false
  };
}
```

11. Now all the tests should pass again and the application should start up without errors.

How it works...

In the preceding section, we introduced a dependency in the `TodosModule` class. As discussed in the *Building and running your first Nancy application (Simple)* recipe, Nancy will instantiate all modules during the application start up and will do so again when a request for a module comes in. In order to instantiate `TodosModule`, Nancy will need an instance of `IDataStore`. This pattern is called Dependency Injection and is well documented elsewhere (for instance, on *Martin Fowlers* bliki `http://www.martinfowler.com/articles/injection.html`). Nancy uses a container to resolve dependencies. The container that Nancy uses by default is `TinyIoC`, and we saw how to set up a dependency with `TinyIoC` in the `bootstrapper` code. The `TinyIoC` container by default supports autowiring by scanning assemblies. This means that without any setup, `TinyIoC` will be able to resolve dependencies in cases where there is only one possible implementation for the dependency.

The `TinyIoC` container can be swapped out further through the `bootstrapper` code. There are a number of NuGet packages with the necessary `bootstrapper` code to use other containers; for instance, Castle Windsor, StructureMap, Autofac, Unity, and Ninject.

There's more...

The bootstrapper allows for much more than just setting up the container. For instance, in the *Adding static content (Intermediate)* recipe, we will use the bootstrapper to set up conventions for locating static files, and in the *Handling cross-cutting concerns – Before, After, and Error Hooks (Intermediate)* recipe, we will use the bootstrapper to set up a pipeline in which we have the custom code running before and after each request handler is executed.

In fact, the bootstrapper allows you to customize just about everything in your Nancy application, including Nancy's internals. We have only scratched the surface in this recipe.

Content negotiation and more model binding (Advanced)

This recipe shows you how to do content negotiation with Nancy. Content negotiation is the mechanism used in HTTP to decide which content type—for example, JSON or XML—to use in response to a request. This involves the client indicating in HTTP Accept headers on the requests as to which content type it prefers and which other ones it can also accept. A browser, for instance, can indicate that it prefers HTML but can also accept X-HTML or XML, whereas a JavaScript application will probably prefer JSON and a mobile app might prefer XML. The server side reads the HTTP Accept headers and chooses the most suitable content type it is capable of responding with. Nancy can handle the server side of this process for you automatically. Out of the box, Nancy is capable of returning JSON, XML, and, as we will see in the next recipe, HTML. On top of this, Nancy makes it easy to plug your own content types to the automatic content negotiation, which we will see towards the end of this recipe where we add support for protocol buffers to our application.

Along the way, we will also make sure that our application accepts the same formats as inputs; that is, the model binding we added in the *Routes and model binding (Intermediate)* recipe works with JSON, XML, and finally protocol buffers.

Getting ready

This recipe builds on the previous recipe, so to follow along you need either your own version of the code from the *Taking a dependency – introducing the bootstrapper (Intermediate)* recipe or the one from the code download.

How to do it...

The following steps show you how to use content negotiation as well as model binding in your Nancy applications:

1. First, we add tests to demonstrate that the model binding already supports XML. Add the following test to `TodoModuleTests`:

```
[Fact]
public void Should_be_able_to_get_posted_xml_todo()
{
  var actual = sut.Post("/todos/", with =>
  {
    with.XMLBody(aTodo);
    with.Accept("application/xml");
  })
  .Then
  .Get("/todos/", with =>
    with.Accept("application/json"));

  var actualBody =
    actual.Body.DeserializeJson<Todo[]>();
  Assert.Equal(1, actualBody.Length);
  Assertions.AreSame(aTodo, actualBody[0]);
}
```

2. This test is very close to a test we already have in the test suite except it performs the action of POSTing a `todo` object as XML instead of a JSON. It also explicitly sets the `Accept` header to indicate `application/json`. This test should pass without changes to the production code.

3. The next step is to add a test for getting back the response from a `GET` `/todos/` HTTP as XML. You can modify the test you just added or you can add this new test—just make sure to set the `Accept` header on the `GET` request to `application/xml` and use XML deserialization to read the response as shown in the following code snippet:

```
[Fact]
public void Should_be_able_to_get_posted_todo_as_xml()
{
  var actual = sut.Post("/todos/", with =>
  {
    with.XMLBody(aTodo);
    with.Accept("application/xml");
  })
  .Then
```

```
  .Get("/todos/", with =>
    with.Accept("application/xml"));

var actualBody =
  actual.Body.DeserializeXml<Todo[]>();
Assert.Equal(1, actualBody.Length);
Assertions.AreSame(aTodo, actualBody[0]);
}
```

4. This test should fail, but to make the test pass, we actually only have to remove a bit of code from our existing `Get` handler; so, it becomes as follows:

```
Get["/"] = _ => todoStore.GetAll();
```

5. When a handler returns an object that is not a Nancy type, Nancy will assume that it is supposed to be serialized into the body of the response and will decide how to do so based on content negotiation.

6. If you re-run all the tests at this point, you will see most of them fail. This is because they do not indicate which content type they accept in responses from our application. To fix this, you will have to go to the tests and add `with.Accept("application/xml")` to each `Get` call to `"/todos/"`. I will leave this as an exercise for you.

7. We also want the `Post` handler in `TodosModule` to use content negotiation, so we add a test to make it capable of returning XML as follows:

```
[Fact]
public void Should_return_created_todo_as_xml_
  when_a_todo_is_posted()
{
  var actual = sut.Post("/todos/",
    with =>
    {
      with.JsonBody(aTodo);
      with.Accept("application/xml");
    });

  var actualBody = actual.Body.DeserializeXml<Todo>();
  Assertions.AreSame(aTodo, actualBody);
}
```

8. This should fail, but to make it pass, we simply need to change the `Post` handler to the following, which tells Nancy to use content negotiation to decide how to serialize the new `todo` object and set the `HTTPStatusCode` to `201 Created` as shown in the following code snippet:

```
Post["/"] = _ =>
{
  var newTodo = this.Bind<Todo>();
  if (newTodo.id == 0)
    newTodo.id = todoStore.Count + 1;

  if (!todoStore.TryAdd(newTodo))
    return HttpStatusCode.NotAcceptable;

  return Negotiate.WithModel(newTodo)
    .WithStatusCode(HttpStatusCode.Created);
};
```

9. I will leave it as an exercise for you to add similar tests for `Put` and for all the combinations of JSON and XML. At the end of this exercise, your `TodosModule` should look like the following code:

```
public class TodosModule : NancyModule
{
  public TodosModule(IDataStore todoStore) :
    base("todos")
  {
    Get["/"] = _ => todoStore.GetAll();

    Post["/"] = _ =>
    {
      var newTodo = this.Bind<Todo>();
      if (newTodo.id == 0)
        newTodo.id = todoStore.Count + 1;

      if (!todoStore.TryAdd(newTodo))
        return HttpStatusCode.NotAcceptable;

      return Negotiate.WithModel(newTodo)
        .WithStatusCode(HttpStatusCode.Created);
    };

    Put["/{id}"] = p =>
    {
      var updatedTodo = this.Bind<Todo>();
```

```
      if (!todoStore.TryUpdate(updatedTodo))
        return HttpStatusCode.NotFound;

      return updatedTodo;
    };

    Delete["/{id}"] = p =>
    {
      if (!todoStore.TryRmove(p.id))
        return HttpStatusCode.NotFound;

      return HttpStatusCode.OK;
    };
  }
}
```

10. So far so good, but now we also want to send `todos` to our application and get them back again using the highly efficient protocol buffer format. The tests for this are similar to the ones you have just added; now, we only need to use the `"application/x-protobuf"` content type and use a protocol buffer's serializer and deserializer.

11. First, add the `protobuf-net NuGet` package to both the `TodosNancy` and `TodosNancyTests` project.

12. Then add the following test to `TodoModuleTests`:

```
[Fact]
public void Should_be_able_to_get_posted
  _todo_as_protobuf()
{
  var actual = sut.Post("/todos/", with =>
  {
    var stream = new MemoryStream();
    Serializer.Serialize(stream, aTodo);
    with.Body(stream, "application/x-protobuf");
     with.Accept("application/xml");
  })
  .Then
  .Get("/todos/", with => with.Accept("application/x-
    protobuf"));

  var actualBody = Serializer.Deserialize<Todo[]>
    (actual.Body.AsStream());
  Assert.Equal(1, actualBody.Length);
  Assertions.AreSame(aTodo, actualBody[0]);
}
```

13. To no surprise, this test fails because we have nothing in our application that can deserialize protocol buffers from an HTTP body or that can serialize an object as protocol buffers into an HTTP body.

14. In order to make the test pass, we add the following two classes to `TodosNancy`: The first class hooks into Nancy's content negotiation and adds support for responding with protocol buffers. The second class hooks into Nancy's model binding and adds support for deserializing protocol buffers from the body of a request into a model object. The key is to implement the `IResponseProcessor` and `IBodyDeserializer` interfaces respectively:

```
public class ProtoBufProcessor : IResponseProcessor
{
  public ProcessorMatch CanProcess(MediaRange
    requestedMediaRange, dynamic model, NancyContext
    context)
  {
    if (requestedMediaRange.Matches(MediaRange.FromString
      ("application/x-protobuf")))
      return new ProcessorMatch { ModelResult =
        MatchResult.DontCare,  RequestedContentTypeResult
        = MatchResult.ExactMatch};

    if (requestedMediaRange.Subtype.ToString()
      .EndsWith("protobuf"))
      return new ProcessorMatch { ModelResult =
        MatchResult.DontCare, RequestedContentTypeResult
        = MatchResult.NonExactMatch };

    return new ProcessorMatch { ModelResult =
      MatchResult.DontCare, RequestedContentTypeResult =
      MatchResult.NoMatch };
  }

  public Response Process(MediaRange requestedMediaRange,
    dynamic model, NancyContext context)
  {
    return new Response
    {
      Contents = stream => Serializer.Serialize(stream,
        model),
      ContentType = "application/x-protobuf"
    };
  }

  public IEnumerable<Tuple<string, MediaRange>>
    ExtensionMappings
```

```
        {
          get { return new[] { new Tuple<string,
            MediaRange>(".protobuf", MediaRange.FromString
            ("application/x-protobuf")) }; }
        }
      }

      public class ProtobufBodyDeserializer : IBodyDeserializer
      {
        public bool CanDeserialize(string contentType)
        {
          return contentType == "application/x-protobuf";
        }
        public object Deserialize(string contentType, Stream
          bodyStream, BindingContext context)
        {
          return Serializer.NonGeneric.Deserialize
            (context.DestinationType, bodyStream);
        }
      }
```

15. Now the test should pass and our application supports three formats—JSON, XML, and protocol buffers—both in and out.

How it works...

Looking at the changes we made in the previous section to the TodosModule class, we see that they are quite small but have a large impact; we went from supporting one format to as many formats as are hooked into Nancy. This is because Nancy handles all the logic involved in content negotiation for us and likewise handles all the logic around picking a deserializer for model binding. In other words, Nancy handles all the looking at HTTP headers and matching them up against registered serializers and deserializers.

In that last part, we saw how amazingly easy it is to add another format to these processes. Note that we made no changes to the TodosModule class whatsoever while adding the support for protocol buffers. All we had to do was to add two classes, each one implementing a rather simple interface. This works because Nancy scans all loaded assemblies during start up and finds all implementations of these interfaces. Nancy can then probe each found implementation in order to find out which content types it can handle; this is what the ProtoBufProcessor.CanProcess, ProtoBufProcessor.ExtensionMappings methods and the ProtobufBodyDeserializer.CanDeserialize methods are for. The information about which content types are handled is returned by these methods and is used by Nancy during model binding and during content negation. If Nancy decides to use the ProtoBufProcessor.Process protocol buffers, ProtobufBodyDeserializer. Deserialize is called.

Adding views (Intermediate)

In this recipe, we will add a couple of Razor views to the application built in the previous recipes. We will see how our module code controls which view to use and how to set up tests for the views.

Getting ready

You need the code built until the *Content negotiation and more model binding (Advanced)* recipe. If you haven't coded along, you can start from the code for the *Content negotiation and more model binding (Advanced)* recipe in the code download.

I will assume you have a working knowledge of Razor, so if you are new to Razor, you should probably brush up on Razor before diving into this recipe.

How to do it...

The following steps will help you add views to your application:

1. As always, we start by adding a test. This test is added to `TodosModuleTests` and does two new things: first, it sets the `Accept` header on the `GET` request to `"text/html"`, which colloquially means "give me back some HTML", and second, it asserts on the contents of the body of the response. The `actual` variable has the `BrowserResponse` type. The `Body` property on `BrowserResponse` objects represents the body of the response from the handler code in the Nancy module. When this body contains HTML, the `BrowserResponse` type supports looking up parts of this HTML using CSS selectors:

```
[Fact]
public void Should_be_able_to_get_view_with_posted_todo()
{
  var actual = sut.Post("/todos/", with =>
  {
    with.JsonBody(aTodo);
    with.Accept("application/json");
  })
  .Then
  .Get("/todos/", with => with.Accept("text/html"));

  actual.Body["title"].ShouldContain("Todos");
  actual.Body["tr#1 td:first-child"]
    .ShouldExistOnce()
    .And
    .ShouldContain(aTodo.title);
}
```

2. The test posts a `Todo` object to our application and then gets it back in the form of HTML. The tests assert that the body of the response to the `GET` request should contain a `title` tag that contains the `"Todos"` text and that the first `td` tag inside the first `tr` tag found in the body should contain the title of the `todo` posted right before.

3. At this point this test fails. Run and see for yourself. Take a look at the error message you get from Nancy. It's a bit long, but it should contain a part similar to the following code:

```
Unable to locate view 'Todo[]'
Currently available view engine extensions: sshtml,html,htm
Locations inspected: views/todos/Todos/Todo[]-da-
DK,views/todos/Todos/Todo[],todos/Todos/Todo[]-da-
DK,todos/Todos/Todo[],views/todos/Todo[]-da-
DK,views/todos/Todo[],todos/Todo[]-da-
DK,todos/Todo[],views/Todos/Todo[]-da-
DK,views/Todos/Todo[],Todos/Todo[]-da-
DK,Todos/Todo[],views/Todo[]-da-DK,views/Todo[],Todo[]-da-
DK,Todo[]Root path: C:\projects\nancy-quick-
start\src\recipe-6\TodoNancy\TodoNancyTests\bin\Debug
```

4. This actually is very useful information. First, it tells us that Nancy is trying to locate a view called `Todo[]`. Second, it tells us which file extensions Nancy expects views to have: `sshtml`, `html`, or `htm`. Third, it tells us all the places Nancy looked for a view in a file called `Todo[]` with one of the listed extensions.

5. The first problem to fix is that we want the view to be called `Todos` and not `Todo[]`. In order to do this, we change the `Get` handler in the `TodosModule` class to this:

```
Get["/"] = _ =>
    Negotiate
    .WithModel(todoStore.GetAll())
    .WithView("Todos");
```

6. The previous code tells Nancy to use content negotiation to control the format of the response and to use `todoStore.GetAll()` as the model; that is, if the request indicates that it accepts JSON, the result of `todoStore.GetAll()` will be serialized to JSON in the body of the response. If the incoming request accepts HTML, Nancy will now look for the `"Todos"` view in all the places indicated in the previous error message, and pass the result of `todoStore.GetAll()` into the view as the model object.

7. As stated in the beginning of the recipe, we want our views to be Razor views, so at this point we install the `Nancy.ViewEngines.Razor` NuGet package in the `TodoNancy` project. This will add references to the `Razor` assembly and the Nancy adaptor for Razor, but in order for Nancy to start using the Razor View Engine, we need to make sure the assembly is loaded. This is done most conveniently on the bootstrapper where we add the following line of code:

```
private RazorViewEngine ensureRazorIsLoaded;
```

8. Now we are ready to add the new `Razor` view. To do so, create a `Views` folder in the `TodoNancy` project, and add an HTML file under the `Views` folder called as `Todos.cshtml`. Then, go to the properties of this new file (either right-click on it in **Solution Explorer** or press *Alt + Enter* while it is selected in **Solution Explorer**) and set the **Copy to Output Directory** property to **Copy always**. Now replace any content in the new `Todos.cshtml` file with the following code snippet:

```
@inherits
Nancy.ViewEngines.Razor.NancyRazorViewBase<TodoNancy.Todo[]>

<html>
  <head><title>Todos</title></head>
  <body>
    <h1>All todos</h1>
    <table>
      <th>Title</th><th>Order</th><th>Completed</th>
      @foreach (var todo in @Model)
      {
        <tr
          id="@todo.id"><td>@todo.title</td><td>
          @todo.order</td><td>@todo.completed</td></tr>
      }
    </table >
    <h1>Add todo</h1>
    <form action="/todos/" method="post">
      <input type="text" name="title" value="title" />
      <input type="number" name="order" value="0" />
      <input type="checkbox" name="completed" />
      <input type="submit" value="add" />
    </form>
  </body>
</html>
```

9. This is a strongly typed Razor view that works on an array of `Todo` objects. It contains a table with a row for each `Todo` object. This is the table we assert on in our test, which should now pass.

10. The `Todos` view also contains a `form` tag that is set up to `post` in `/todos/`. In the code download for this recipe, you will find a test for this form, but I will leave it out here because it is similar to the tests we added previously.

11. Try to run the application and go to /todos in your browser. You should see the Todos view showing whatever views you have in your implementation of todoStore. You should also see the form, but if you fill in the form and click on **add**, you get an Internal Server Error. If you look at the details of the error, you will see that Nancy cannot locate an appropriate view to use. To fix this, add a test that does a POST and accepts text/html and then change the handler for Post in TodosModule as shown in the following code snippet:

```
Post["/"] = _ =>
{
  var newTodo = this.Bind<Todo>();
  if (newTodo.id == 0)
    newTodo.id = todoStore.Count + 1;

  if (!todoStore.TryAdd(newTodo))
    return HttpStatusCode.NotAcceptable;

  return Negotiate.WithModel(newTodo)
    .WithStatusCode(HttpStatusCode.Created)
    .WithView("Created");
};
```

12. For this to work, we need to add another view called Created.cshtml. I will leave it up to you to implement the Created view (or you can look in the code download).

There's more...

Nancy doesn't support Razor views alone; out of the box, Nancy comes with Super Simple View Engine, which—as the name indicates—is a simple (yet fairly powerful) view engine with a syntax akin to Razor. The Super Simple View Engine expects files to have the .sshtml extension, which is why this particular extension is listed when Nancy can't find a view.

Furthermore, there are NuGets for various other view engines such as Spark, Nustache, and others.

As is always the case with Nancy, you can also roll on your own if you cannot find support for your favorite view engine. In order to do this, you basically implement the IViewEngine interface against your favorite view engine and let Nancy automatically wire your new view engine up with the rest of the framework.

Adding static content (Intermediate)

So far we have focused on dynamic content. Our handlers in the `TodosModule` project have returned either data or views that depended on the data in our data store and the data in the request.

In this recipe, we look at how to serve static content. This can be images, icons, CSS files, JavaScript files, and plain old HTML files.

Getting ready

This recipe builds on the code from the previous recipe, so have your copy of that ready. If you have not coded along, you can start off from the code for the *Adding views (Intermediate)* recipe in the code download.

How to do it...

The following steps show how to add static content in your application:

1. First note that the code in the code download already has static content since the *Routes and model binding (Intermediate)* recipe, where the `backbone.js` based todo SPA was added as a client to our `TodoNancy` server-side application. The `backbone.js` todo SPA consists of the `index.htm` file in the `Views` folder and a bunch of JavaScript of CSS files in the `Content` folder. The `index.htm` view is returned from the `HomeModule` class and is therefore handled as dynamic content. The files in the `Content` folder on the other hand are not returned by any handlers in any Nancy modules. They are just served directly by Nancy. We have done nothing special to make this work. We just rely on Nancy—by convention—to consider everything in the `Content` folder to be static content and make it available through HTTP `GET` requests to `/Content/{path-to-file}`.

2. Since `TodoNancy` is first and foremost an API, we want to provide documentation for it. To this end, we want to serve some static HTML files from `/docs`. Add a new file, `DocumentationTests`, to the `TodoNancyTests` project, and add the following test to it:

    ```
    [Fact]
    public void Should_give_access_to_overview
      _documentation()
    {
      var sut = new Browser(new Bootstrapper());

      var actual = sut.Get("/docs/overview.htm", with =>
        with.Accept("text/html"));
    ```

```
        Assert.Equal(HttpStatusCode.OK, actual.StatusCode);
    }
```

3. This simply checks that our application accepts requests for `text/html` to `/docs/ overview.htm` and responds with a `200 OK` status code. Right now the test fails. To make it pass, we need to do a few things. First, we add a `Docs` folder and a `Docs/ overview.htm` file to the `TodoNancy` project. You can put whatever HTML you want in the new file as it doesn't matter; for instance, the following code will do:

```
<html>
<head>
    <title>Todo Nancy API Overview</title>
</head>
<body>
 ... documentation would go here ...
</body>
</html>
```

4. Make sure the `Copy to Output Directory` property for `overview.htm` is set to `Copy Always`.

5. Second, we add a custom convention that tells Nancy to treat anything inside `Docs` as static content. Add the following code to `bootstrapper`:

```
    protected override void ConfigureConventions
        (NancyConventions conventions)
    {
        base.ConfigureConventions(conventions);

        conventions.StaticContentsConventions.Add(
        StaticContentConventionBuilder.AddDirectory("/docs",
            "Docs")
        );
    }
```

6. This accesses the list of conventions for where to find static content and adds an extra convention. In other words, the default Nancy convention is preserved alongside our custom convention. Our convention is built using the `StaticContentConventionBuilder` helper API. This allows to easily build conventions for static content folders and for individual static content files. More involved schemes can also be created by coding up a convention by hand.

7. Re-run the test and watch it pass. If you want you can also point your browser to `/ Docs/overview.htm`.

There's more...

Nancy makes a lot of things easy by providing reasonable conventions out of the box. One of these conventions is that files in /Content are considered as static content. We saw how to augment this convention with our own convention in the override of ConfigureConventions in the bootstrapper code. This bootstrap method similarly allows for setting up custom conventions; for example, you can view locations and culture in case the default conventions do not suit you.

Hosting Nancy on the Cloud (Intermediate)

In this recipe, we take a look at how to host the application we have written so far on cloud services, such as on Windows Azure and AppHarbor. Both of these have PaaS solutions for running ASP.NET applications on their cloud infrastructure. In both cases, the application we've written so far is capable of running except for two things mentioned as follows:

▶ The connection string for the data store has to be moved out of the code and into web.config. Hardcoding, as I have done so far, is a really bad idea, so moving the connection string to the web.config file is good anyway.

▶ Avoid running the integration tests during the cloud build.

Getting ready

As always, we build on the code from the previous recipe, so just have that ready.

How to do it...

The following steps will help you host the application you built on cloud services:

1. First go to AppHarbor (https://appharbor.com) and; just create an account with a free plan, since that should be fine for playing around with.

2. Follow the instructions on the AppHarbor website to create an application, but do not deploy your Nancy application yet.

3. Assuming that we are using MongoDB for the implementation of the IDataStore interface, add the MongoLab add-on to your AppHarbor application. This gives you access to a cloud-hosted MongoDB database that we will have our AppHarbor-hosted TodosNancy run against. If you have chosen another database for the data store, have a look through the AppHarbor add-ons—chances are there is an add-on for your type of database.

4. Go to the `web.config` file in `TodosNancy` and add the following line to the application settings section:

```
<appSettings>
  <add key="webPages:Enabled" value="false" />
  <add key="MONGOLAB_URI"
    value="mongodb://localhost:27017/todos"/>
</appSettings>
```

5. Then change the `bootstrapper` class to use this configuration value while connecting to the database as follows:

```
protected override void ConfigureApplicationContainer
  (TinyIoCContainer container)
{
  base.ConfigureApplicationContainer(container);

  var connectionString = ConfigurationManager.
    AppSettings.Get("MONGOLAB_URI");
  var mongoDataStore = new MongoDataStore
    (connectionString);
  container.Register<IDataStore>(mongoDataStore);
}
```

6. For all the tests to still pass, add an `app.config` file to the `TodosNancyTests` project and add the corresponding settings to it:

```
<configuration>
  <appSettings>
    <add key="MONGOLAB_URI" value="mongodb://localhost:27017/
todos"/>
  </appSettings>
</configuration>
```

7. The last piece missing before being ready to deploy this to AppHarbor is make sure the integration tests, that is, the tests in `DocumentationTests` and `TodosModuleTest`, are not run during the AppHarbor build and deploy pipeline. The reason for this is that we, on the one hand, want to take advantage of the fact that AppHarbor will run all unit tests it sees and only deploy if the tests pass, but on the other hand, we do not want to mess with setting up a test database on the cloud that can be used during test runs in AppHarbor. Note that if you use SQL Server for your data store, the xUnit `AutoRollback` attribute can be used to roll back changes made in tests. In real life scenarios (especially continuous delivery scenarios), though, you will probably want to do that test setup and have all the tests run in AppHarbor before deploying. To avoid running the integration tests on the cloud, first write an implementation of the `ITestClassCommand` interface in xUnit.net that only allows tests to run if they are running on a known developer machine and then apply it to the integration tests. The implementation is as follows:

```
public class KnownDevMachinesOnly : ITestClassCommand
{
  private TestClassCommand command;
  private ITypeInfo typeInf;

  public int ChooseNextTest(ICollection<IMethodInfo>
    testsLeftToRun)
  {
    return command != null ? command.ChooseNextTest
      (testsLeftToRun) : -1;
  }

  public Exception ClassFinish()
  {
    return command != null ? command.ClassFinish() :
      null;
  }

  public Exception ClassStart()
  {
    return command != null ? command.ClassStart() : null;
  }

  public IEnumerable<ITestCommand>
    EnumerateTestCommands(IMethodInfo testMethod)
  {
    return command != null ?
      command.EnumerateTestCommands(testMethod) : new
      ITestCommand[0];
  }

  public IEnumerable<IMethodInfo> EnumerateTestMethods()
  {
    return command != null ?
      command.EnumerateTestMethods() : new
      IMethodInfo[0];
  }

  public bool IsTestMethod(IMethodInfo testMethod)
  {
    return command != null ?
      command.IsTestMethod(testMethod) : false;
  }

  public object ObjectUnderTest
```

```
    {
      get { return command != null ?
        command.ObjectUnderTest : null; }
    }

    public ITypeInfo TypeUnderTest
    {
      get { return typeInf; }
      set
      {
        typeInf = value;
        if (KnowDevMachineNames.Contains
          (Environment.MachineName))
          command = new TestClassCommand(value);
      }
    }

    public IEnumerable<string> KnowDevMachineNames
    {
      get
      {
        yield return "HORSDAL";
        yield return "DEV2";
      }
    }
}
```

8. Then apply it to the tests by adding an attribute that indicates to xUnit.net that it should use our custom `KnownDevMachinesOnly` class when trying to run the tests as shown in the following code:

```
[RunWith(typeof(KnownDevMachinesOnly))]
public class TodosModuleTests

[RunWith(typeof (KnownDevMachinesOnly))]
public class DocumentationTests
```

9. The only steps left now are to follow AppHarbors instructions on how to deploy the application. I will not repeat those here.

How it works...

AppHarbor is built for automatically running ASP.NET application. So, as long as our Nancy application is also an ASP.NET application, AppHarbor can run it. Since we have chosen to use the `Nancy.Hosting.Aspnet` NuGet package, our application runs on top of ASP.NET; so, from AppHarbor's standpoint, it is just an ASP.NET application.

There's more...

Nancy applications can also run easily on Windows Azure. With the slight modifications we have done in this recipe, the application is almost ready to run on Azure. The remaining bit is to make our application connect to the MongoDB document database once deployed to Azure. The easiest way to do this is to take advantage of `Web.config` transformations and add a `Web.Release.config` file containing the connection string to use in Azure. In fact, AppHarbor also supports `Web.config` transformations; so, this feature gives a solution that works in both cloud services.

Once the connection string issue is under control, just follow the instructions for deploying an ASP.NET MVC application to Windows Azure. The options for doing this include deploying from within Visual Studio using DropBox, TFS, Git, and more. All of these deployment paths work with Nancy applications too.

Handling cross-cutting concerns – Before, After, and Error hooks (Intermediate)

In this recipe, we take a look at how to handle cross cutting concerns in our Nancy application. Specifically, we will see the following:

▶ Use the before and after hooks to log every incoming request and to log all the status codes of all responses

▶ Use the error hook to log all unhandled exception from our modules

Both of these are achieved via the application wide hooks; that is, they work for all requests. There are similar module specific hooks; for example, they work only on requests handled by that module.

We will use the NLog (`http://nlog-project.org`) logging library in this recipe but this could be any logging library.

Getting ready

We will work on the code done so far. So open up your copy of the code from the previous recipe, or get a copy of it from the code download.

How to do it...

The following steps help you understand how to hook into Nancy's request pipeline:

1. Install the NLog NuGet package to both the `TodoNancy` and `TodoNancyTests` projects.

2. Add a new C# file to the `TodoNancyTests` project and call it `RequestLoggingTests.cs`.

3. Add tests that check if requests, status codes, and exceptions are logged. We achieve this by overriding the NLog configuration such that all log messages are written to an object in memory. This enables us to assert that the log entries we expect have been written. The test code you need looks as follows:

```csharp
public class RequestLoggingTests
{
    private Browser sut;
    private MemoryTarget actualLog;
    private const string infoRequestlogger =
        "|INFO|RequestLogger";
    private const string errorRequestlogger =
        "|ERROR|RequestLogger";

    public RequestLoggingTests()
    {
        sut = new Browser(new Bootstrapper());
        OverrideNLogConfiguration();
    }

    private void OverrideNLogConfiguration()
    {
        actualLog = new MemoryTarget();
        actualLog.Layout += "|${exception}";
        SimpleConfigurator.ConfigureForTargetLogging
            (actualLog, LogLevel.Info);
    }

    [Theory]
    [InlineData("/")]
    [InlineData("/todos/")]
    [InlineData("/shouldnotbefound/")]
    public void ShouldLogIncomingRequests(string path)
    {
        sut.Get(path);

        Assert.True(TryFindExptedInfoLog(actualLog, "Handling
            request GET \"" + path + "\""));
    }

    [Theory]
    [InlineData("/", HttpStatusCode.OK)]
```

```
[InlineData("/todos/", HttpStatusCode.OK)]
[InlineData("/shouldnotbefound/",
  HttpStatusCode.NotFound)]
public void ShouldLogStatusCodeOffResponses(string
  path, HttpStatusCode expectedStatusCode)
{
  sut.Get(path);

  Assert.True(TryFindExptedInfoLog(actualLog,
    "Responding " + expectedStatusCode +" to GET \"" +
    path + "\""));
}


[Fact]
public void ShouldLogErrorOnFailingRequest()
{
  try
  {
    sut.Delete("/todos/illegal_item_id");
  }
  catch {}
  finally
  {
    Assert.True(TryFindExptedErrorLog(actualLog, "Input
      string was not in a correct format."));
  }
}

private static bool TryFindExptedInfoLog(MemoryTarget
  actualLog, string expected)
{
  return TryFindExptedLogAtExpectedLevel(actualLog,
    expected, infoRequestlogger);
}

private static bool TryFindExptedErrorLog(MemoryTarget
  actualLog, string expected)
{
  return TryFindExptedLogAtExpectedLevel(actualLog,
    expected, errorRequestlogger);
}

private static bool TryFindExptedLogAtExpectedLevel
  (MemoryTarget actualLog, string expected, string
  requestloggerLevel)
```

```
{
  var tryFindExptedLog =
    actualLog.Logs
      .Where(s => s.Contains(requestloggerLevel))
      .FirstOrDefault(s => s.Contains(expected));
  if (tryFindExptedLog != null)
    return true;

  Console.WriteLine("\"{0}\" not found in log filtered
    by \"{1}\":", expected, requestloggerLevel);
  Console.WriteLine(actualLog.Logs.Aggregate
    ("[\n\t{0}\n]", (acc, s1) => string.Format(acc, s1
    + "\n\t{0}")));
  return false;
}
}
```

4. To make these tests pass, we need to hook into Nancy before each request, after each request, and on errors. We do this in the bootstrapper by adding handlers to the `Before`, `After`, and `OnError` pipelines. We also go a little bit ahead and add NLog configuration, even though we do not have tests for it, by adding the following code to our bootstrapper:

```
private Logger log = LogManager.GetLogger
  ("RequestLogger");

protected override void ApplicationStartup
  (TinyIoCContainer container, IPipelines pipelines)
{
  base.ApplicationStartup(container, pipelines);

  SimpleConfigurator.ConfigureForTargetLogging(new
    AsyncTargetWrapper(new EventLogTarget()));

  LogAllRequests(pipelines);
  LogAllResponseCodes(pipelines);
  LogUnhandledExceptions(pipelines);
}

private void LogAllRequests(IPipelines pipelines)
{
  pipelines.BeforeRequest += ctx =>
  {
    log.Info("Handling request {0} \"{1}\"",
      ctx.Request.Method, ctx.Request.Path);
```

```
        return null;
    };
}

private void LogAllResponseCodes(IPipelines pipelines)
{
    pipelines.AfterRequest += ctx =>
        log.Info("Responding {0} to {1} \"{2}\"",
            ctx.Response.StatusCode, ctx.Request.Method,
            ctx.Request.Path);
}

private void LogUnhandledExceptions(IPipelines
    pipelines)
{
    pipelines.OnError.AddItemToStartOfPipeline
        ((ctx, err) =>
    {
        log.ErrorException(string.Format("Request {0}
            \"{1}\" failed", ctx.Request.Method,
            ctx.Request.Path), err);
        return null;
    });
}
```

5. The tests should now pass and when you run the application log entries, they should be written to the Windows Event Log.

6. As an exercise, first add tests for POST, PUT, and DELETE requests. Then add a test, which first makes a request that doesn't cause any exceptions and then checks that no logging error occurred.

How it works...

Nancy sets up a pipeline to which all requests are sent through. At the center of the pipeline is the actual handler for the request. The pipeline hooks, we have seen, allows you to do things before the request reaches the handler and after the handler has returned a response, as well as doing other things in case the handler throws an exception.

In the hooks, we have access to NancyContext—the ctx variable in the previous code—which means that we have access to everything there is to know about the request: the HTTP method used, if it had form values, the body contents, the headers present, the module that handled it, the body of the response, the status code, the headers on the response, and so on.

In the previous code for the `Before` hook, we return `null`. This tells Nancy to keep running the pipeline. If on the other hand we return a `Response`, we implicitly tell Nancy that the request has now been handled and the response returned from the `Before` hook will be the response to the request. Similarly, we can return a `Response` from the `OnError` hook and have that sent back to the client allowing us to; for example, presenting custom error pages.

There's more...

As mentioned at the beginning of this recipe there are similar `Before`, `After`, and `OnError` hooks that work on individual modules instead of the whole application.

Specifically for logging, it is worth noting that you can use ELMAH (`http://code. google.com/p/elmah`) with Nancy. Just install the `Nancy.Elmah` NuGet package and call `ElmahLogging.Enable` during the application start up. This will use the `After` and `OnError` hooks to set up ELMAH logging.

Authenticating users (Intermediate)

In this recipe, we extend the `TodoNancy` application to provide users with the option of logging in with Twitter. If users are logged in, they can read, modify, and delete their own Todos. Users—with the exception of anonymous users—will not be able to see each other's todos. Just like up until this point, any user can walk up to `TodoNancy` and add todos. If they are not authenticated, the application sees them as anonymous users and pools all their todos together in one big bucket belonging to the anonymous user.

Getting ready

As usual, open the code from the last recipe or grab it from the code download. Either way, you should be ready for the steps in this recipe as soon as you have the code from the last recipe.

How to do it...

The following steps help you add an authentication to your Nancy applications:

1. First we introduce a simple `User` class in `TodoNancy` and along with it a special anonymous user:

```
namespace TodoNancy
{
  using System.Collections.Generic;
  using Nancy.Security;

  public class User : IUserIdentity
  {
```

```
    public static IUserIdentity Anonymous { get; private
      set; }
    static User()
    {
      Anonymous = new User { UserName = "anonymous" };
    }

    public string UserName { get; set; }
    public IEnumerable<string> Claims { get; private set; }
  }
}
```

2. Install the third-party NuGet package called `Nancy.Authentication.`
`WorldDomination`. This package provides integration of the `WorldDomination`
library into Nancy. WorldDomination provides an easy API towards third-party public
authentication services, such as Facebook, Google, and Twitter. We are only going to
take advantage of the Twitter part, but the code for setting up Google and Facebook
login with WorldDomination is similar to that for Twitter.

3. The WorldDomination Nancy integration works by providing handlers that take care of
the communication with the third-party authentication services. These handlers can
be reached simply by linking to them. In order to grant Twitter the access to log in in
our application, we simply add the following line of code to `Todos.cshtml`:

```
<a href="/authentication/redirect/twitter">Login with
  Twitter</a>
```

4. When users click on this link, they are redirected to Twitter where they can log in
and authorize our application to access their Twitter ID. When this process is done,
WorldDomination calls back to a hook in our application code where we can do
whatever application-specific stuff we need. In our case, we want to do two things:
set a cookie containing an access token and redirect to `"/"`. We specify these two
things in a couple of tests that we put in a new class in `TodoNancyTests` called
`AuthenticationTests`, which I will not go into detail with, since it has more to do
with WorldDomination than with Nancy:

```
[Fact]
public void Should_redirect_to_root_on_social
  _authc_callback()
{
  new Browser(new Bootstrapper()).Get("/testing");
  var callbackData = new AuthenticateCallbackData
  {
    AuthenticatedClient = new AuthenticatedClient("")
    {
      UserInformation = new UserInformation { UserName
        = "chr_horsdal" }
```

```
        }
    };

    var sut = new SocialAuthenticationCallbackProvider();

    var actual = sut.Process(TestingModule.actualModule,
        callbackData);

    Assert.Equal(HttpStatusCode.SeeOther,
        actual.StatusCode);
}

[Fact]
public void Should_set_todo_user_cookie_on_social
    _authc_callback()
{
    new Browser(new Bootstrapper()).Get("/testing");
    var userNameToken = new TokenService().GetToken
        ("chr_horsdal");
    var callbackData = new AuthenticateCallbackData
    {
        AuthenticatedClient = new AuthenticatedClient("")
        {
            UserInformation = new UserInformation { UserName
                = "chr_horsdal" }
        }
    };

    var sut = new SocialAuthenticationCallbackProvider();

    var actual = (Response) sut.Process(TestingModule
        .actualModule, callbackData);

    Assert.Contains("todoUser", actual.Cookies.Select
        (cookie => cookie.Name));
    Assert.Contains(userNameToken, actual.Cookies.Select
        (cookie => cookie.Value));
}
```

5. To make these tests pass—well even just compile—add this class to `TodoNancy`:

```
public class SocialAuthenticationCallbackProvider :
    IAuthenticationCallbackProvider
{
    public dynamic Process(NancyModule module,
        AuthenticateCallbackData callbackData)
```

```
{
    module.Context.CurrentUser = new User { UserName =
        callbackData.AuthenticatedClient
        .UserInformation.UserName };
    return module.Response
        .AsRedirect("/")
        .AddCookie(new NancyCookie("todoUser", new
            TokenService().GetToken(module.Context.
            CurrentUser.UserName)));
}

public dynamic OnRedirectToAuthenticationProviderError
    (NancyModule nancyModule, string errorMessage)
{
    return "login failed: " + errorMessage;
}
}
```

6. The key thing in the previous code is that the
SocialAuthenticationCallbackProvider class implements the
IAuthenticationCallbackProvider interface, which is defined by
WorldDomination. WorldDomination automatically picks up the implementation of
IAuthenticationCallbackProvider and uses it for the callbacks at the end
of the authentication process. There is one callback used for error cases and one
used for successful cases. In the successful cases, we pick the username out of the
callback data, obtain an access token for that user, and set a cookie with the token.
Finally, we redirect to the root of our application. The access token is obtained from
a service that I'm not showing here. This service has the responsibility to provide
secure tokens, authenticate them later on, to revoke them if necessary, and possibly
time them out after a period of inactivity. The details of this are beyond the scope
of this book. Nota Bene. The implementation of the TokenService in the code
download is just the identity function, which is very insecure and should not be used
in production.

7. At this point, users can authenticate with Twitter and we store an access token in
a cookie on their machine, but we forget all about that when they make their next
request. So, the next step is to read the cookie on incoming requests and to set the
current user based on the contents. The first test towards this is as follows:

```
[Fact]
public void Should_set_user_identity_
    when_cookie_is_set()
{
    var expected = "chr_horsdal";
    var userNameToken = new
        TokenService().GetToken(expected);
```

```
    var sut = new Browser(new Bootstrapper());

    sut.Get("/testing", with => with.Cookie("todoUser",
      userNameToken));

    Assert.Equal(expected, TestingModule.
      actualUser.UserName);
}
```

8. The previous test makes a request to /testing, which is a route picked up by a test module that we add to TodoNancy testing. The testing module remembers the current user when it receives a request:

```
public class TestingModule : NancyModule
{
  public static IUserIdentity actualUser;
  public TestingModule()
  {
    Get["/testing"] = _ =>
    {
      actualUser = Context.CurrentUser;
      return HttpStatusCode.OK;
    };
  }
}
```

9. As an exercise, add a similar test that checks that the current user is set to the anonymous user when no todoUser cookie is set.

10. To set the current user on incoming requests, we add a Before action by calling the following method in the Bootstrapper.ApplicationStartup method:

```
private static void SetCurrentUserWhenLoggedIn
  (IPipelines pipelines)
{
  pipelines.BeforeRequest += context =>
  {
    if (context.Request.Cookies.
      ContainsKey("todoUser"))
      context.CurrentUser = new TokenService().
        GetUserFromToken(context.Request.
        Cookies["todoUser"]);
    else
      context.CurrentUser = User.Anonymous;
    return null;
  };
}
```

11. This just looks at the request to see if there is a `"todoUser"` cookie. If so, the `TokenService` method is asked to resolve the access token to a user, otherwise the anonymous user is used. Note that anything we set on NancyContext in a `Before` action is carried through to the handler and any `After` actions.

12. The user can now log in and we remember the log in for as long as the access token is valid. We are still not doing anything based on the current user though. What we want to do is to let the user have a private set of todos. To spec this out, we need to add tests for HTTP requests to `/todos` using the `GET`, `POST`, `PUT`, and `DELETE` verbs and using different combination of usernames. For the sake of brevity, I have only included one such test here. The rest I am sure you can easily write at this point:

```csharp
public class UserSpecificTodosTests
{
  private const string UserName = "Alice";
  private readonly Browser sut;
  private readonly IDataStore fakeDataStore;

  public UserSpecificTodosTests()
  {
    fakeDataStore = A.Fake<IDataStore>();
    sut = new Browser(with =>
    {
      with.Module<TodosModule>();
      with.ApplicationStartup((container, pipelines) =>
      {
        container.Register(fakeDataStore);
        pipelines.BeforeRequest += ctx =>
        {
          ctx.CurrentUser = new User { UserName =
            UserName };
          return null;
        };
      });
    });
  }

  [Theory]
  [InlineData(0, 0, 0)] [InlineData(0, 10,
    0)] [InlineData(0, 0, 10)] [InlineData(0, 10, 10)]
  [InlineData(1, 0, 0)] [InlineData(1, 10,
    0)] [InlineData(1, 0, 10)] [InlineData(1, 10, 10)]
  [InlineData(42, 0, 0)] [InlineData(42, 10,
    0)] [InlineData(42, 0, 10)] [InlineData(42, 10, 10)]
```

```
public void Should_only_get_user_own_todos(int
  nofTodosForUser, int nofTodosForAnonymousUser, int
  nofTodosForOtherUser)
{
  var todosForUser = Enumerable.Range(0,
    nofTodosForUser).Select(i => new Todo { id = i,
    userName =  UserName });
  var todosForAnonymousUser = Enumerable.Range(0,
    nofTodosForAnonymousUser).Select(i => new Todo { id
    = i });
  var todosForOtherUser = Enumerable.Range(0,
    nofTodosForOtherUser).Select(i => new Todo { id =
    i, userName = "Bob" });

  A.CallTo(() => fakeDataStore.GetAll())
   .Returns(todosForUser.Concat(todosForAnonymousUser)
    .Concat(todosForOtherUser));

  var actual = sut.Get("/todos/", with =>
    with.Accept("application/json"));

  var actualBody =
    actual.Body.DeserializeJson<Todo[]>();
  Assert.Equal(nofTodosForUser, actualBody.Length);
}
```

13. These tests drive changes to our `TodosModule`, the `IDataStore` interface, and the `MongoDatastore` class such that the module inspects the current user, and the module and data store in concert provide access to only the users own todos. The `IDatastore` interface becomes as follows:

```
public interface IDataStore
{
  IEnumerable<Todo> GetAll();
  long Count { get; }
  bool TryAdd(Todo todo);
  bool TryRmove(int id, string userName);
  bool TryUpdate(Todo todo, string userName);
}
```

14. And the `TodosModule` class becomes as follows (the changes are highlighted):

```
public class TodosModule : NancyModule
{
  public TodosModule(IDataStore todoStore) :
    base("todos")
```

```
{
  Get["/"] = _ =>
    Negotiate
    .WithModel(todoStore.GetAll().Where(todo =>
      todo.userName == Context.CurrentUser.UserName)
      .ToArray())
    .WithView("Todos");

  Post["/"] = _ =>
  {
    var newTodo = this.Bind<Todo>();
    newTodo.userName = Context.CurrentUser.UserName;
    if (newTodo.id == 0)
      newTodo.id = todoStore.Count + 1;

    if (!todoStore.TryAdd(newTodo))
      return HttpStatusCode.NotAcceptable;

    return Negotiate.WithModel(newTodo)
                    .WithStatusCode(HttpStatusCode.Created)
                    .WithView("Created");
  };

  Put["/{id}"] = p =>
  {
    var updatedTodo = this.Bind<Todo>();
    updatedTodo.userName = Context.CurrentUser.UserName;
    if (!todoStore.TryUpdate(updatedTodo, Context.CurrentUser.
      UserName))
      return HttpStatusCode.NotFound;

    return updatedTodo;
  };

  Delete["/{id}"] = p =>
  {
    if (!todoStore.TryRmove(p.id, Context.CurrentUser.
      UserName))
      return HttpStatusCode.NotFound;

    return HttpStatusCode.OK;
  };
  }
}
```

How it works...

Most of what we did in the preceding steps we have seen before. The main new part is the `WorldDomination` library. Simply by installing the Nancy.Authentication.WorldDomination NuGet package, we got a few new routes and handlers in our Nancy application. WorldDomination achieves this by taking advantage of the way Nancy discovers modules. Nancy scans all loaded assemblies for implementations of `INancyModule`. This scanning includes third-party assemblies, so the Nancy integration in WorldDomination simply includes Nancy modules, which then automatically become part of our application.

There's more...

Nancy also supports authentication controlled directly in the application. For instance, there is a NuGet package that provides forms authentication, and there is another NuGet supporting stateless authentication schemes.

For modules that we only want to allow authenticated users to access, Nancy provides a convenience method; just add the following line of code to the constructor and all unauthenticated requests to the module are denied access:

```
this.RequiresAuthentication();
```

Similarly, if you only want to allow HTTPS requests, just add the following line of code:

```
this.RequiresHttps();
```

Note that the `User` class we previously introduced includes a list of claims. We did not take advantage of these but it shows that Nancy supports adding claims-based authorization. We just have to make the `TokenService` type provide a list of claims for the user and then check them in the modules. Nancy provides even more convenient methods for checking claims. For instance, `RequiresClaims` accepts a list of claims. If the current user does not have those claims, the access is denied.

Separating applications and hosting (Advanced)

In this recipe, we see how Nancy separates your application from where it is running. Not only is this a nice separation of concerns but also it allows you to write a Nancy application once, and then go run it in a number of different ways; for example, inside a WPF application, a Windows Service, on top of Katana, on Mono, or on top of ASP.NET.

We will take our `TodoNancy` application and pull all the application code out of the ASP.NET project into a separate class library. We will then create a console application and set it up to host our Nancy application. The end result is that we have one Nancy application that we can run either inside a console application or on top of ASP.NET. In fact, we can have it running on both simultaneously as long as we use different ports for different instances.

Getting ready

Open up the code from the last recipe. As always, if you have not been coding along, you can get a copy of the code from the *Authenticating users (Intermediate)* recipe from the code download.

How to do it...

The following steps help you structure your Nancy application such that it can run under multiple hosts:

1. To accommodate having one Nancy application that we can host in two different ways, we need to do a little bit of restructuring. Looking at the **Solution Explorer** in Visual Studio, we want to end up with this structure:

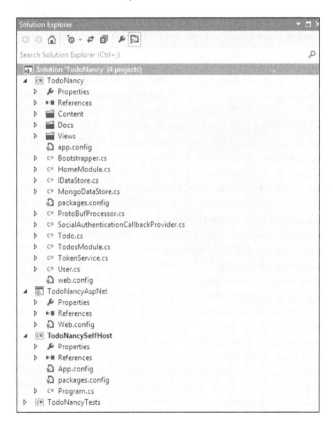

2. In the previous screenshot, all the application code is in the **TodoNancy** project, the ASP.NET hosting is in the **TodoNancyAspNet**, and the self-hosting is in the **TodoNancySelfHost**. First step towards this structure is to rename the current `TodoNancy` project to `TodoNancyAspNet` and also to rename the corresponding file system folder as `TodoNancy`.

3. Create a new class library called `TodoNancy` and move all code in the files from `TodoNancyAspNet` except `web.config` and `packages.config` to it.

4. Install the Nancy, Nancy.Authentication.WorldDomination, Nancy.ViewEngines.Razor, NLog, mongocsharpdriver, and protobuf-net NuGet packages in `TodoNancy`.

5. Uninstall the Nancy.Authentication.WorldDomination, Nancy.ViewEngines. Razor, NLog, mongocsharpdriver, and protobuf-net NuGet packages from `TodoNancyAspNet`.

6. Add a project reference from `TodoNancyAspNet` to `TodoNancy`.

7. At this point, the solution should compile, all tests should run, and the application should work if you run the `TodoNancyAspNet` project. Try it out.

8. Create a new console application called `TodoNancySelfHost`.

9. Install the Nancy.Hosting.Self NuGet in `TodoNancySelfHost`.

10. Add a project reference from `TodoNancySelfHost` to `TodoNancy`.

11. Add the following code to `program.cs` in `TodoNancySelfHost`:

```
namespace TodoNancySelfHost
{
    using System;
    using Nancy.Hosting.Self;
    using TodoNancy;

    class Program
    {
        static void Main(string[] args)
        {
            TodosModule artificiaReference;
            var nancyHost = new NancyHost(new
                Uri("http://localhost:8080/"));
            nancyHost.Start();

            Console.ReadKey();

            nancyHost.Stop();
        }
    }
}
```

12. Add the following code to `app.config` in `TodoNancy`:

```
<appSettings>
  <add key="MONGOLAB_URI" value="mongodb://localhost:27017/
todos"/>
</appSettings>
```

13. The only thing left to do is to make the self-hosted version work, which allows your user to listen on `locahost:8080`. You can do this with the following `netsh` command:

```
PS C:\> netsh http add urlacl url=http://+:8080/
user=DOMAIN\USERNAME
```

14. If you run the `TodoNancySelfHost` project and go to `localhost:8080`, you should see the familiar `TodoNancy` application.

Using async handlers (Advanced)

In this recipe, we make one of the handlers in the `TodosModule` project asynchronous. Doing so is relevant for any handler that makes the current thread wait for something during processing—typically some sort of I/O. This could be a call to an external service, file access, or, as in our case, access to a database. Think about the deployment to AppHarbor we did in the *Hosting Nancy on the Cloud (Intermediate)* recipe. The Nancy application is on AppHarbor, but the MongoDB database is on another service. This means that whenever our handlers' call the database, it incurs a remote call, which in turn means that the thread will be waiting a while for the response. A lot of the times, we don't notice this wait, but nonetheless it means that we have a thread sitting around doing nothing for a while. If we make the database call asynchronously, the thread could do something else meanwhile. If we make the whole handler asynchronous, the thread could even process another request while the database call is pending.

At the time of writing, this feature of Nancy has not reached the final release, so we will be switching over to using a beta release. This means that the code shown here may well need to be changed if you are running on a later and final version of the Nancy async features.

Getting ready

As usual, just grab your copy of the code from the last recipe, and you are ready to start this one.

How to do it...

1. In order to install the Nancy async beta with NuGet, we need to add the feed from
    `https://www.myget.org/F/nancyasync/` as a source in the package manager
    in Visual Studio.

2. Next, update the Nancy NuGet package to the newest beta version. This will
    add async support to Nancy. In order to update to a beta version, include the
    `IncludePrerelease` option in the NuGet command:

    ```
    PM> Update Nancy -IncludePrerelease
    ```

3. Run all tests to see if updating the Nancy package had any negative effects. The
    `RequestLoggingTests.Should_log_error_on_failing_request` test will
    fail because the error pipeline is now async. Due to the way in which .NET handles
    propagating exceptions in async code, `FormatException` we are expecting to log
    is wrapped inside `AggregateExcption`. We can get the error logging we want by
    changing just one line in the bootstrapper as follows:

    ```
    private void LogUnhandledExceptions(IPipelines pipelines)
    {
      pipelines.OnError.AddItemToStartOfPipeline((ctx, err) =>
      {
        log.ErrorException(string.Format("Request {0}
          \"{1}\" failed. Exception: {2}",
        ctx.Request.Method, ctx.Request.Path,
        err.ToString()), err);
        return null;
      });
    }
    ```

4. We are now ready to take advantage of async in our route handlers, so we go into the
    `TodosModule` project and change the handler for `"/"` to the following:

    ```
    Get["/", true] = async (_, __) =>
    {
      var allTodos = await todoStore.GetAll();
      return Negotiate
        .WithModel(allTodos.Where(todo => todo.userName
          == Context.CurrentUser.UserName).ToArray())
        .WithView("Todos");
    };
    ```

5. We changed the signature of the delegate handling the route and also added an extra parameter to the route. We will get back to these changes in the following *How it works...* section. For now, we need to compile the code again. That is, we need to make the `todosStore.GetAll()` call return a `Task`. The `IDataStore` interface becomes as follows:

    ```
    public interface IDataStore
    {
      Task<IEnumerable<Todo>> GetAll();
      long Count { get; }
      bool TryAdd(Todo todo);
      bool TryRmove(int id, string userName);
      bool TryUpdate(Todo todo, string userName);
    }
    ```

6. As an exercise, you now have to update your implementation of `IDataStore` accordingly. The updated version of the `MongoDataStore` class is in the code download for this recipe. Furthermore, you will need to update a few tests that fake out the call as we just made async. In each of these tests, the fake return values have to be wrapped in the `Task` objects and these tasks need to be started. As an example, look at the following test from `DataStoreTests`:

    ```
    [Fact]
    public void Should_remove_deleted_todo_from_datastore()
    {
      var returnValue = new Task<IEnumerable<Todo>>(() =>
        new [] { new Todo { id = 1 }, new Todo { id = 2 }
        });
      returnValue.Start();
      A.CallTo(() => fakeDataStore.GetAll())
        .Returns(returnValue);

      sut.Delete("/todos/1");

      A.CallTo(() => fakeDataStore.TryRmove(1,
        A<string>._)).MustHaveHappened();
    }
    ```

7. When you have made similar changes to all tests, they should all pass again, and the application should work just like it used to except now one of our handlers is asynchronous.

How it works...

Let's take another look at the handler for GET "/todos/:

```
Get["/", true] = async (_, __) =>
{
  var allTodos = await todoStore.GetAll();
  return Negotiate
    .WithModel(allTodos.Where(todo => todo.userName ==
      Context.CurrentUser.UserName).ToArray())
    .WithView("Todos");
};
```

The first thing to notice is that the signature of the handler changed from a lambda taking one argument to a lambda taking two arguments. The first argument is the same dynamic parameter argument as before where we made the handler async. The second argument is a cancellation token. The cancellation token is of the System.Threading.CancellationToken type and is a standard part of programming with .NET Task<T> objects. The cancellation token is used to propagate notifications to tasks if they are to be cancelled.

The second thing to notice is that there are now two arguments to the indexer on Get. The first argument is the route as usual, but the second argument is new. The second argument is either a Boolean expression or a Func<NancyContext, bool> argument. In both the cases, the second argument tells Nancy whether the handler should be executed asynchronously or not. Using a Func<NancyContext, bool> argument allows your code to inspect the NancyContext for each individual request before deciding whether or not to handle it asynchronously, giving your application code quite fine-grained control. In our case, we have simply decided upfront to always do async handling.

There's more...

Handlers for other HTTP methods apart from GET can also be asynchronous and so can Before, After, and OnError hooks. Each of these is made async in a similar fashion to how our handler for GET "/todos/" was made async. All in all, it is straightforward to make your Nancy applications completely async if you want and if your application logic does not rely on being executed synchronously.

Thank you for buying
Instant Nancy Web Development

About Packt Publishing

Packt, pronounced 'packed', published its first book "*Mastering phpMyAdmin for Effective MySQL Management*" in April 2004 and subsequently continued to specialize in publishing highly focused books on specific technologies and solutions.

Our books and publications share the experiences of your fellow IT professionals in adapting and customizing today's systems, applications, and frameworks. Our solution based books give you the knowledge and power to customize the software and technologies you're using to get the job done. Packt books are more specific and less general than the IT books you have seen in the past. Our unique business model allows us to bring you more focused information, giving you more of what you need to know, and less of what you don't.

Packt is a modern, yet unique publishing company, which focuses on producing quality, cutting-edge books for communities of developers, administrators, and newbies alike. For more information, please visit our website: www.packtpub.com.

Writing for Packt

We welcome all inquiries from people who are interested in authoring. Book proposals should be sent to author@packtpub.com. If your book idea is still at an early stage and you would like to discuss it first before writing a formal book proposal, contact us; one of our commissioning editors will get in touch with you.

We're not just looking for published authors; if you have strong technical skills but no writing experience, our experienced editors can help you develop a writing career, or simply get some additional reward for your expertise.

Microsoft .NET Framework 4.5 Quickstart Cookbook

ISBN: 978-1-849686-98-3   Paperback: 226 pages

Get up to date with the exciting new features in NET 4.5 Framework with these simple but incredibly effective recipes

1. Designed for the fastest jump into .NET 4.5, with a clearly designed roadmap of progressive chapters and detailed examples.

2. A great and efficient way to get into .NET 4.5 and not only understand its features but clearly know how to use them, when, how and why.

3. Covers Windows 8 XAML development, .NET Core (with Async/Await & reflection improvements), EF Code First & Migrations, ASP.NET, WF, and WPF

Ext.NET Web Application Development

ISBN: 978-1-849693-24-0   Paperback: 410 pages

A guide to building Rich Internet Applications with Ext. NET using ASP.NET Web Forms and ASP.NET MVC

1. Build rich internet applications using the power of Ext.NET controls

2. Learn how Ext.NET leverages Sencha's popular Ext JS JavaScript framework to provide a full client-server web development experience

3. Full of examples and tips, with clear step-by-step instructions

Please check **www.PacktPub.com** for information on our titles

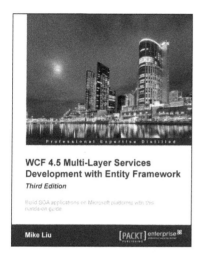

**WCF 4.5 Multi-Layer Services
Development with Entity Framework**

WCF 4.5 Multi-Layer Services
Development with Entity Framework
Third Edition

Build SOA applications on Microsoft platforms with this
hands-on guide

Mike Liu

WCF 4.5 Multi-Layer Services Development with Entity Framework

ISBN: 9781-849687-66-9   Paperback: 394 pages

Build SOA applications on Microsoft platforms with this
hands-on guide

1. This book will teach you WCF, Entity Framework,
   LINQ, and LINQ to Entities quickly and easily.

2. Apply best practices to your WCF services and
   utilize Entity Framework in your WCF services.

3. Practical, with step-by-step instructions and
   precise screenshots, this is a truly hands-on book
   for all C++, C#, and VB.NET developers.

**.NET 4.5 Extension
Methods How-to**

Utilize and harness the power of extension methods in your
.NET applications

Shawn R. McLean

Instant .NET 4.5 Extension Methods How-to

ISBN: 978-1-849688-56-7   Paperback: 52 pages

Utilize and harness the power of extension methods in
your .NET applications

1. Learn something new in an Instant! A short, fast,
   focused guide delivering immediate results.

2. Explains how to write your own extension methods
   on types ranging from primitive to complex

3. Shows caveats to watch out for and apply
   workarounds to them

Please check **www.PacktPub.com** for information on our titles